Come Rejoice!

Edited by Michael Perry

WORDS EDITION

Jubilate Hymns
Marshall Pickering

William Collins Sons & Co. Ltd.
London · Glasgow · Sydney · Auckland
Toronto · Johannesburg

First published in Great Britain in 1990 by Marshall Pickering

Marshall Pickering is an imprint of
Collins Religious Division,
part of the Collins Publishing Group
8 Grafton Street, London W1X 3LA

Copyright © 1990 Michael Perry

Text set by Barnes Music Engraving Ltd., East Sussex, England
Printed in the UK by Sussex Litho Limited, Chichester

ISBN 0 551 02059 8

Music Edition ISBN 0 551 01948 4

Contents

Preface

The Jubilate group, as it has come to be known, was founded in the early 1960's by Michael Baughen (now Bishop of Chester) and friends closely involved in work among young people. The group pooled their talents to meet the challenge of a new generation who wished to extend their singing beyond the foursquare ways of metrical hymnody, and the unpredictability of Anglican chant!

Initially, no publisher could be found to support the first joint enterprise, *Youth Praise* (1966). The Church Pastoral Aid Society came to the rescue, later publishing *Youth Praise 2* (1969), and *Psalm Praise* (1973) which was a contemporary effort to revitalise the use of Psalms. *Youth Praise* was a best-seller in its time and *Psalm Praise* goes on and on . . .

As the work on *Psalm Praise* got under way, the group comprised Michael Baughen (by this time at All Souls' Church, Langham Place), Richard Bewes (who later succeded him as Rector), Christopher Collins, Timothy Dudley-Smith (who afterwards became Bishop of Thetford), Christopher Idle, Gavin Reid, Edward Shirras, Michael Perry, Michael Saward, James Seddon, Norman Warren, and David Wilson – a mixed bunch of talent, in terms of words and music.

In the mid-1970's an enlarged section of the group under Michael Baughen's leadership (most of whom are represented in this volume) began to apply themselves to the production of a pioneering modern language hymnal[1]. After years of conference and dedication, *Hymns for Today's Church* was born in 1982. *HTC* now sells in seven separate editions.

About this time, George Shorney of Hope Publishing in Carol Stream, Illinois, USA, enlisted the cooperation, first of Timothy Dudley-Smith, and then of the extended Jubilate Hymns group. His was a far-sighted move towards mutual enrichment of the USA and UK repertoires[2]. Thus Jubilate and their works have found their way into USA hymnals – *Worship*, *Rejoice in the Lord*, *The Hymnal 1982*, *Psalter Hymnal*, and others. Similarly, American hymns are beginning to emerge in Jubilate publications.

Jubilate authors and musicians – there are now forty of them – differ remarkably in their style, taste and approach. Since the major figures among them are all friends, and can take firm criticism from one another, there is a considerable strength in their working together. Their breadth of style is also reflected in a variety of Jubilate publications: *Church Family Worship* (1986 and 1988), *Carols for Today* (1986), *Carol Praise* (1987), *Let's Praise* (1988), *The Wedding Book* (1989), and *Psalms for Today* and *Songs from the Psalms* (1990).

This present collection *Come Rejoice!* illustrates their *hymn* style, and includes some of their most popular combinations of words and music, as well as a cluster of previously unpublished works which the editor believes will be gladly received by the churches. As well as their mutual love of hymnody, Jubilate authors and musicians share a confidence in the future of church music and an energising faith in the Spirit of God who brings life to human offerings of talent and devotion.

Michael Perry

---

[1] See: *Hymns in Today's Language*, Christopher Idle, Grove Books, Bramcote, Nottingham, UK; 1982.

[2] See: *The Hymnal Explosion in North America*, George H Shorney, Hope Publishing Company, Carol Stream, Illinois 60188; 1988.

1
From Psalm 95, Joel 2 etc.
© Michael Perry/Jubilate Hymns

1 Blow upon the trumpet!
clap your hands together,
sound aloud the praises of the Lord
    your king.
God has kept the promise,
granting us salvation:
let the people jubilantly shout and sing!

2 Blow upon the trumpet!
let the nations tremble;
see what power obliterates
    the sun and moon.
This is God's own army
bringing all to judgement,
for the day of Jesus Christ is coming soon.

3 Blow upon the trumpet!
Arrows in the lightning
fly the storm of battle
    where we march along.
Glory to our shepherd
keeping us through danger,
setting us like jewels in a royal crown!

4 Blow upon the trumpet!
Christ is surely coming,
heaven's forces mobilizing at his word.
We shall rise to meet him:
death at last is conquered,
God gives us the victory
    through Christ our Lord!

2
From Psalm 50
© David Mowbray/Jubilate Hymns

1 Let God, who called the worlds to be,
arise in all-consuming fire
to judge the people righteously,
and faithless ones with awe inspire.

2 This God is ours, and yet we break
the covenant made long ago;
God's words we foolishly forsake,
God's ways we have refused to know.

3 For though our lips
    have preached God's law,
our erring hearts have scorned the Name;
we choose the thief and slanderer
as friends, and so increase our shame.

4 What then shall God the Lord demand?
Not gifts or lavish offering,
but vows and promises performed,
and lives from which true praises spring!

3
From Psalm 49
© Michael Perry/Jubilate Hymns

1 O people, listen –
    hear God's wisdom crying!
Although the darkness
    comes to rich and poor,
and nothing mortal
    can survive our dying,
yet in the morning
    justice shall endure:

2 For God will take the holy
    into heaven,
by grace redeem the faithful
    from the grave;
we leave behind us
    all this world has given,
and trust God's mighty power
    to love and save!

3 To Father, Son and Spirit
    be the glory!
Come, worship and adore
    the holy Name;
let wisdom think upon
    our human story,
and faith
    our ever-living God proclaim.

4
© Christopher Idle/Jubilate Hymns

1 Now let us learn of Christ:
he speaks, and we shall find
he lightens our dark mind;
so let us learn of Christ.

2 Now let us love in Christ
as he has first loved us;
as he endured the cross,
so let us love in Christ.

3 Now let us grow in Christ
and look to things above,
and speak the truth in love;
so let us grow in Christ.

4 Now let us stand in Christ
in every trial we meet,
in all his strength complete;
so let us stand in Christ.

5

1 Had he not loved us
he had never come,
yet is he love
and love is all his way;
low to the mystery
of the virgin's womb
Christ bows his glory –
born on Christmas Day.

2 Had he not loved us
he had never come;
had he not come
he need have never died
nor won the victory
of the vacant tomb,
the awful triumph
of the crucified.

3 Had he not loved us
he had never come;
still were we lost
in sorrow, sin and shame,
the doors fast shut
on our eternal home
which now stand open –
for he loved and came.

6

1 Jesus, child of Mary born,
Son of God and Lord most high;
come to wear a crown of thorn,
bravely come to die.

2 To this place of pain and fear
love descends in human guise;
God in Christ self-emptied here,
foolishness most wise:

3 Infant in a manger laid,
wrapped about with peasant shawl;
gift of grace so freely made,
saviour for us all.

4 Angel hosts the skies adorn,
we with shepherds glorify
Jesus, child of Mary born,
Son of God most high.

7

1 Holy child, how still you lie!
safe the manger, soft the hay;
faint upon the eastern sky
breaks the dawn of Christmas Day.

2 Holy child, whose birthday brings
shepherds from their field and fold,
angel choirs and eastern kings,
myrrh and frankincense and gold:

3 Holy child, what gift of grace
from the Father freely willed!
In your infant form we trace
all God's promises fulfilled.

4 Holy child, whose human years
span like ours delight and pain;
one in human joys and tears,
one in all but sin and stain:

5 Holy child, so far from home,
all the lost to seek and save,
to what dreadful death you come,
to what dark and silent grave!

6 Holy child, before whose name
powers of darkness faint and fall;
conquered, death and sin and shame –
Jesus Christ is Lord of all!

7 Holy child, how still you lie!
safe the manger, soft the hay;
clear upon the eastern sky
breaks the dawn of Christmas Day.

8

1 When things began to happen,
before the birth of time,
the Word was with the Father
and shared his holy name;
without him there was nothing –
all life derives from him;
his light shines in the darkness –
an unextinguished beam.

2 He came to his creation,
the work of his own hand;
he entered his own country
but they would not respond:
yet some gave their allegiance
of life and heart and mind;
thus they became his subjects
and he became their friend.

3 Conceived by heaven's mercy,
    there was no human birth;
    for they are God's own children
    redeemed from sin and death:
    and they beheld his glory,
    so full of grace and truth;
    in Christ, God's Son, our saviour,
    whom we adore by faith.

After P Gerhardt (1607–1676)
C Winkworth (1827–1878)
© in this version Word & Music/Jubilate Hymns

9

1 All my heart this night rejoices,
    as I hear,
        far and near,
    sweetest angel voices.
    'Christ is born!' their choirs are singing,
        till the air
        everywhere
    now with joy is ringing.

2 Listen! from a humble manger
        comes the call,
        'One and all,
    run from sin and danger!
    Christians come, let nothing grieve you:
        you are freed!
        All you need
    I will surely give to you.'

3 Gather, then, from every nation;
        here let all,
        great and small,
    kneel in adoration;
    love him who with love is yearning:
        Hail the star
        that from far
    bright with hope is burning!

4 You, my Lord, with love I'll cherish,
        live to you,
        and with you
    dying, shall not perish,
    but shall dwell with you for ever:
        joy divine
        shall be mine
    that can alter never.

10 From Isaiah 9
© Pearl Beasley/Jubilate Hymns

1 A child is born for us today,
    a son to us is given;
    the saviour comes to guide our way
    and lead us up to heaven.
        They'll call him 'Wonderful',
        heavenly 'Counsellor'.
    We'll call him 'Jesus'.

2 He comes to be the 'Prince of peace',
    to all the world a friend;
    his mighty love will never cease,
    his kingdom will not end.
        They'll call him 'Mighty God',
        'Eternal Father'.
    We'll call him 'Jesus'.

3 On those who walk the darkest way
    has dawned a shining light
    far brighter than the brightest day,
    a great and glorious sight.
        O come, Emmanuel,
        our God, be with us!
    O come, Lord Jesus!

11 After E. Flèchier (1632–1710)
© Michael Perry/Jubilate Hymns

1 Child in a stable:
    how lovely is this place
        where God is able
    to show such perfect grace!
    No princely babe that smiled
    or palace that beguiled,
        in history or fable,
    could ever match this child
        within a stable.

2 God comes in weakness,
    and to our world for love
        descends with meekness
    from realms of light above.
    This Child shall heal our wrong,
    for sorrow give a song,
        and hope in place of bleakness;
    for nothing is so strong
        as God in weakness.

3 Now night is ended!
    the chasm that divides
        at last is mended,
    and God with us abides.
    For on this happy morn
    new glory wakes the dawn;
        the Sun is high ascended –
    to us a child is born,
        and night is ended!

12 © Michael Perry/Jubilate Hymns

1 Christ is born to be our king –
listen, as the angels sing,
to the heavens echoing,
   'Glory be to God on high!'

2 Shepherds in the fields at night
hear the tidings, see the light,
find the child, in praise unite:
   'Glory be to God on high!'

3 Christians down the ages tell
Christ can break the powers of hell,
so that we may sing as well,
   'Glory be to God on high!'

13 © Michael Perry/Jubilate Hymns

1 Come and hear the joyful singing,
   Alleluia, gloria,
set the bells of heaven ringing:
   alleluia, gloria,
God the Lord has shown us favour –
   alleluia, gloria,
Christ is born to be our saviour.
   alleluia, gloria!

2 Angels of his birth are telling,
   Alleluia, gloria,
prince of peace all powers excelling;
   alleluia, gloria,
death and hell can not defeat him:
   alleluia, gloria,
go to Bethlehem and greet him.
   alleluia, gloria!

3 Choir and people, shout in wonder,
   Alleluia, gloria,
let the merry organ thunder;
   alleluia, gloria,
thank our God for love amazing,
   alleluia, gloria,
Father, Son and Spirit praising.
   alleluia, gloria!

14 © Michael Perry/Jubilate Hymns

1 Come and sing the Christmas story
   this holy night!
Christ is born: the hope of glory
   dawns on our sight.
Alleluia! Earth is ringing
with a thousand angels singing –
hear the message they are bringing
   this holy night.

2 Jesus, saviour, child of Mary
   this holy night,
in a world confused and weary
   you are our light.
God is in a manger lying,
manhood taking, self denying,
life embracing, death defying
   this holy night.

3 Lord of all! Let us acclaim him
   this holy night;
king of our salvation name him,
   throned in the height.
Son of Man – let us adore him:
all the earth is waiting for him;
Son of God – we bow before him
   this holy night.

15 © Christopher Porteous/Jubilate Hymns

1 I see your crib –
a cradle where the cattle cry,
and in the stall you lie,
sweet Mary's holy boy.
The promise, and the love, God gives –
yet in the world around
no place for him is found.
'No room!' they cried –
our Lord was left outside.

2 I see your face,
so full of love in sleep –
and shepherds leave their sheep
to come and worship here.
Good news, which choirs of angels tell,
God's only, wondrous Son
to us on earth has come.
See where he lies in straw;
gaze, worship, and adore!

3 I see your star –
a guide, the way for men and kings,
the gift of God who brings
salvation for our sins,
to grow in grace with God and man.
He had no home, no bed:
'Come, follow me!' he said –
Lord, let me hear your call,
and bring my life, my all!

16 © Michael Perry/Jubilate Hymns

1 Lift your heart and raise your voice;
faithful people, come, rejoice:
grace and power are shown on earth
in the saviour's holy birth.
Gloria!

2 Mortals, hear what angels say;
shepherds, quickly make your way,
finding truth in lowly guise,
wisdom to confound the wise.
Gloria!

3 Here he lies, the Lord of all;
nature's king in cattle-stall,
God of heaven to earth come down –
cross for throne and thorn for crown.
Gloria!

4 Lift your hearts and voices high:
then shall glory fill the sky,
Christ shall come and not be long,
earth shall sing the angels' song:
'Gloria!'

17 © Paul Wigmore/Jubilate Hymns

1 Mary came with meekness,
Jesus Christ to bear,
laid the Lord of glory in a manger there.
We come rejoicing,
Jesus Christ to love:
baby in a manger –
king of heaven above!

2 Angels came with praises,
Jesus Christ to name,
heaven's choirs exalting
him who bears our shame.
We come rejoicing . . .

3 Shepherds came with trembling,
Jesus Christ to see;
king who, at their bidding
would their shepherd be.
We come rejoicing . . .

4 Wise men came with treasure,
Jesus Christ to bless –
he who shares all blessings
heaven and earth possess.
We come rejoicing . . .

18 From the German
© Paul Wigmore/Jubilate Hymns

1 O come all you children
to Bethlehem town,
and see here a baby
from heaven come down;
tread softly and enter on this sacred night
a stable with heavenly glory alight.

2 O come all you children,
come here to the stall
and see here a child
who is born Lord of all;
more fair than the angels in glory is he,
more lovely than cherubim ever could be.

3 O come all you children,
and stand by his bed,
and see gentle Mary bend low at his head;
see Joseph, so humble in wondering joy,
kneel down at the feet
of this most holy boy.

4 O come then you children,
and hark at the throng
of angels, all crowding the sky
with their song;
join in with their praises and joyfully sing
your loudest thanksgiving –
for Jesus the King!

19 © Michael Perry/Jubilate Hymns

1 See him lying on a bed of straw:
a draughty stable with an open door;
Mary cradling the babe she bore –
the prince of glory is his name.
O now carry me to Bethlehem
to see the Lord of love again:
just as poor as was the stable then,
the prince of glory when he came.

2 Star of silver, sweep across the skies,
show where Jesus in the manger lies;
shepherds, swiftly from your stupor rise
to see the saviour of the world!
O now carry . . .

3 Angels, sing again the song you sang,
sing the glory of God's gracious plan;
sing that Bethl'em's little baby can
be the saviour of us all.
O now carry . . .

4 Mine are riches, from your poverty,
   from your innocence, eternity;
   mine forgiveness by your death for me,
   child of sorrow for my joy.
      O now carry me to Bethlehem
      to see the Lord of love again:
      just as poor as was the stable then,
      the prince of glory when he came.

20 Based on the Latin
        © Michael Perry/Jubilate Hymns

1 Sleep, Lord Jesus! Mary smiling
   on her infant so beguiling
      sings a joyful lullaby.

2 Sleep, Lord Jesus! Mary grieving
   at the fate our sin is weaving
      sings a solemn lullaby.

3 Sleep, Lord Jesus! Mary dreaming
   of this fallen world's redeeming
      sings a holy lullaby.

   Sleep, Lord Jesus, lullaby!

21 © Michael Perry/Jubilate Hymns

   Ring out the bells –
   the joyful news is breaking;
   ring out the bells
   for Jesus Christ is born!

1 Angels in wonder
      sing of his glory;
   shepherds returning
      tell us the story.
   Ring out . . .

2 Let all creation
      worship before him;
   earth bring him homage,
      heaven adore him!
   Ring out . . .

3 Prophets have spoken –
      hark to their warning:
   shadows are passing,
      soon comes the morning!
   Ring out . . .

22 © Michael Perry/Jubilate Hymns

ALL
1 When God from heaven
      to earth came down
      on Christmas Day, on Christmas Day,
   the songs rang out in Bethlehem town
      on Christmas Day in the morning.

WOMEN AND GIRLS
2 For Christ was born to save us all,
      on Christmas Day, on Christmas Day,
   and laid within a manger stall
      on Christmas Day in the morning.

MEN AND BOYS
3 The shepherds heard the angels sing
      on Christmas Day, on Christmas Day,
   to tell them of the saviour-king
      on Christmas Day in the morning.

ALL
4 Now joy is ours and all is well,
      on Christmas Day, on Christmas Day,
   so sound the organ, chime the bell
      on Christmas Day in the morning!

23 © Paul Wigmore/Jubilate Hymns

1 Small wonder the star,
      small wonder the light,
   the angels in chorus,
      the shepherds in fright;
   but stable and manger for God –
   no small wonder!

2 Small wonder the kings,
      small wonder they bore
   the gold and the incense,
      the myrrh, to adore;
   but God gives his life on a cross –
   no small wonder!

3 Small wonder the love,
      small wonder the grace,
   the power, the glory,
      the light of his face;
   but all to redeem my poor heart –
   no small wonder!

24 From Luke 2 (*The Song of Simeon/Nunc dimittis*)
        J E Seddon (1915–1983)
        © Mrs M Seddon/Jubilate Hymns

1 Lord, now let your servant
      go his way in peace;
   your great love has brought me
      joy that will not cease:

2 For my eyes have seen him
      promised from of old –
   saviour of all people,
      shepherd of one fold:

3 Light of revelation
      to the gentiles shown,
   light of Israel's glory
      to the world made known.

25 From Psalm 100 (*Jubilate Deo*)
© Michael Baughen/Jubilate Hymns

1 Come, rejoice before your maker
all you peoples of the earth;
serve the Lord your God with gladness,
come before him with a song!

2 Know for certain that Jehovah
is the true and only God:
we are his, for he has made us;
we are sheep within his fold.

3 Come with grateful hearts before him,
enter now his courts with praise;
show your thankfulness towards him,
give due honour to his name.

4 For the Lord our God is gracious –
everlasting in his love;
and to every generation
his great faithfulness endures.

26 © Brian Hoare/Jubilate Hymns

1 Born in song!
God's people have always been singing.
Born in song!
hearts and voices raised.
So today we worship together:
God alone is worthy to be praised.

2 Christ is king!
he left all the glory of heaven.
Christ is king!
born to share in our pain;
crucified, for sinners atoning;
risen, exalted, soon to come again.

3 Sing the song!
God's Spirit is poured out among us.
Sing the song!
God has made us anew;
every member part of the Body,
given his power, his will to seek and do.

4 Tell the world!
all power to Jesus is given.
Tell the world!
he is with us always.
Spread the word, that all may receive him;
every tongue confess and sing his praise.

5 Then the end!
Christ Jesus shall reign in his glory.
Then the end
of all earthly days.
Yet above, the song will continue;
all his people still shall sing his praise!

27 © Michael Saward/Jubilate Hymns

1 Welcome to another day!
Night is blinded:
'Welcome', let creation say;
darkness ended.
Comes the sunshine after dew,
time for labour;
time to love my God anew
and my neighbour.

2 Welcome to the day of prayer
with God's people;
welcome is the joy we share
at this table.
Bread and wine from heaven fall:
come, receive it
that the Christ may reign in all
who believe it.

3 Welcome is the peace that's given,
sure for ever;
welcome is the hope of heaven
when life's over.
As we work and as we pray,
trust God's story:
come then, as the dawning day
heralds glory!

28 After Alcuin (c735–804)
© Christopher Idle/Jubilate Hymns

1 Eternal light, shine in my heart,
eternal hope, lift up my eyes;
eternal power, be my support,
eternal wisdom, make me wise.

2 Eternal life, raise me from death,
eternal brightness, help me see;
eternal Spirit, give me breath,
eternal Saviour, come to me:

3 Until by your most costly grace,
invited by your holy word,
at last I come before your face
to know you, my eternal God.

29 From *Phos hilaron* (*Hail Gladsome Light*)
© Christopher Idle/Jubilate Hymns

1 Light of gladness, Lord of glory,
Jesus Christ our king most holy,
shine among us in your mercy:
earth and heaven join their hymn.

2 Let us sing at sun's descending
as we see the lights of evening,
Father, Son, and Spirit praising
with the holy seraphim.

3 Son of God, through all the ages
  worthy of our holiest praises,
  yours the life that never ceases,
    light which never shall grow dim.

6 All on earth who serve our God,
  priests and people of the Lord,
  upright, holy, humble hearts:
    worship, all creation.

30 From *Te lucis ante terminum*
(At the ending of the day)
© Michael Perry / Jubilate Hymns

1 Now evening comes to close the day,
  and soon the silent hours
  shall banish all our fears away,
  and sleep renew our powers.

2 Into your hands, eternal Friend,
  we give ourselves again,
  and to your watchful care commend
  all those in grief or pain.

3 In waking, lift our thoughts above,
  in sleeping guard us still,
  that we may rise to know your love
  and prove your perfect will.

4 To Father, Son and Spirit – praise,
  all mortal praise be given,
  till sleep at last shall end our days
  and we shall wake in heaven!

31 From *A song of creation / Benedicite*
© Judy Davies / Jubilate Hymns

1 Bless the Lord, created things,
  highest heavens, angel host;
  bless the Father, Spirit, Son:
    worship, all creation.

2 Sun and moon and stars of heaven,
  showery waters, rain and dew,
  stormy gale and fiery heat:
    worship, all creation.

3 Scorching wind and bitter cold,
  icy blizzard, morning mist,
  light and darkness, nights and days:
    worship, all creation.

4 Frosty air and falling snow,
  clouds and lightnings, dales and hills,
  all that grows upon the earth:
    worship, all creation.

5 Springs and rivers, ocean deeps,
  whales and fishes of the sea,
  prowling beasts and soaring birds:
    worship, all creation.

32 © David Mowbray / Jubilate Hymns

1 Lord of the changing year,
  patterns and colours bright;
  all that we see and hear,
  sunrise and starlit night:
  the seasons, Lord in splendour shine,
  your never-failing wise design.

2 Lord of the winter scene,
  hard-frozen ice and snow;
  death where once life has been,
  nothing is seen to grow;
  few creatures roam, few birds will fly
  across the clouded Christmas sky:

3 Lord of unfolding spring,
  promise of life to come;
  nature begins to sing
  where once her tongue was dumb;
  the crocus blooms, the hedgerows wake,
  and Easter day is soon to break:

4 Lord of the summer days,
  spreading and green the trees;
  songthrush lifts high your praise,
  gulls light on deep-blue seas;
  the warmth and welcome of the sun
  brings happiness to everyone:

5 Lord of the autumn gold,
  reaping and harvest home,
  sheep safely in the fold,
  turn of the year has come:
  the seasons, Lord in splendour shine,
  your never-failing wise design.

33 From Psalm 104, for Family von Rad
© Michael Perry / Jubilate Hymns

1 The majesty of mountains,
  the sovereignty of skies,
  the regal rocks that arch above
  where veils of vapour rise,
  are gifts of God, the Lord of love,
  the worshipful, the wise.

2 The running of the river,
  the surging of the sea,
  the grass that grows, high on the hill,
  the flower and fruiting tree,
  our Saviour sends us, by whose will
  all creatures came to be.

3 The glory of the Godhead,
   the Spirit and the Son,
   the Father, faithful down the days:
   to them, the Three-in-One,
   while life shall last be perfect praise
   and highest honour done!

3 Be their delight in joy,
        their hope in sorrow,
   be their true friend in pleasure as in pain;
   guest of today and guardian of tomorrow,
   turn humble water into wine again!

34
J E Seddon (1915–1983)
© Mrs M Seddon/Jubilate Hymns

1 Jesus the Lord of love and life,
   draw near to bless this man and wife;
   as they are now in love made one,
   let your good will for them be done.

2 Give them each day your peace and joy,
   let no dark clouds these gifts destroy;
   in growing trust may love endure,
   to keep their marriage-bond secure.

3 As they have vowed to have and hold,
   each by the other be consoled;
   in wealth or want, in health or pain,
   till death shall part, let love remain.

4 Deepen, O Lord, their love for you,
   and in that love, their own renew;
   each in the other find delight,
   as lives and interests now unite.

5 Be to them both a guide and friend,
   through all the years their home defend;
   Jesus the Lord of love and life,
   stay near and bless this man and wife.

35
© Michael Perry/Jubilate Hymns

1 Lord Jesus Christ,
        invited guest and saviour,
   with tender mercy hear us as we pray;
   grant our desire
        for those who seek your favour,
   come with your love
        and bless them both today.

2 Give them your strength
        for caring and for serving,
   give them your graces –
        faithfulness and prayer;
   make their resolve to follow you
        unswerving,
   make their reward
        your peace beyond compare.

36
© David Mowbray/Jubilate Hymns

1 Where may that love be found
   uplifting and complete,
   a love which bears and braves all things,
   which death cannot defeat?

2 A parent for its child
   will often mountains move;
   a husband caring for a wife
   reflects this strength of love.

3 In Christ upon the Cross
   Love's depths we see revealed;
   a sacrifice for others' sake,
   as God the Father willed.

4 No greater love than this
   dare we expect to find,
   that seeks the good of the beloved
   and leaves self-love behind.

5 Give us, Lord Christ, your help
   to tread this narrow way,
   to live your resurrection life
   and enter into joy.

37
From Psalm 69
© Michael Perry/Jubilate Hymns

1 When the waters cover me,
        save me, O God;
   when I look and cannot see,
   when I seek what cannot be,
   when my friends abandon me,
        save me, O God.

2 You know all my guilty fears,
        thank you, O God,
   you have heard with open ears,
   you have seen my contrite tears,
   you will bless me all the years –
        thank you, O God.

38/39
From Psalm 28
© Michael Perry/Jubilate Hymns

1 O Lord, my rock, to you I cry
when others will not hear;
to you I lift my hands on high –
your arms are always near.

2 I grieve for those who keep fine friends
but harbour Godless schemes;
who use your works for worthless ends,
to squander on their dreams.

3 Yet praise the Lord –
who comes at length,
who comes to right the wrong:
to you our shepherd and our strength
be praise in joyful song!

40
From Psalm 91
© Timothy Dudley-Smith

1 Safe in the shadow of the Lord,
beneath his hand and power,
I trust in him,
I trust in him,
my fortress and my tower.

2 My hope is set on God alone
though Satan spreads his snare;
I trust in him,
I trust in him
to keep me in his care.

MEN
3 From fears and phantoms of the night,
from foes about my way,
I trust in him,
I trust in him,
by darkness as by day.

WOMEN
4 His holy angels keep my feet
secure from every stone;
I trust in him,
I trust in him,
and unafraid go on.

5 Strong in the everlasting name,
and in my Father's care,
I trust in him,
I trust in him,
who hears and answers prayer.

6 Safe in the shadow of the Lord,
possessed by love divine,
I trust in him,
I trust in him,
and meet his love with mine.

41
From The Lord's Prayer
J E Seddon (1915–1983)
© Mrs M Seddon/Jubilate Hymns

1 Father God in heaven,
Lord most high:
hear your children's prayer,
Lord most high:
hallowed be your name,
Lord most high –
O Lord, hear our prayer.

2 May your kingdom come
here on earth;
may your will be done
here on earth,
as it is in heaven
so on earth –
O Lord, hear our prayer.

3 Give us daily bread
day by day,
and forgive our sins
day by day,
as we too forgive
day by day –
O Lord, hear our prayer.

4 Lead us in your way,
make us strong;
when temptations come
make us strong;
save us all from sin,
keep us strong –
O Lord, hear our prayer.

5 All things come from you,
all are yours –
kingdom, glory, power,
all are yours;
take our lives and gifts,
all are yours –
O Lord, hear our prayer.

42
From Psalm 84
© Barbara Woollett/Jubilate Hymns

1 How lovely is your dwelling-place!
O Lord most high,
We long to know more of your grace,
and yearn to see you face to face,
O Lord most high!

2 The sparrow comes to build her nest
O Lord most high,
and in your house finds peace and rest:
so may we too be ever blessed,
O Lord most high!

3 Your people come to you again,
　　O Lord most high,
　for here we feel your strength like rain
　refreshing us through toil and pain,
　　O Lord most high!

4 In fellowship your love we share,
　　O Lord most high;
　far better is one day of prayer
　than any spent in worldly care,
　　O Lord most high!

5 How lovely is your dwelling-place!
　　O Lord most high;
　we bring you all our trust and praise,
　and ask your blessing on our days,
　　O Lord most high!

43 © Michael Perry/Jubilate Hymns

1 Like a mighty river flowing,
　like a flower in beauty growing,
　far beyond all human knowing
　　is the perfect peace of God.

2 Like the hills serene and even,
　like the coursing clouds of heaven,
　like the heart that's been forgiven
　　is the perfect peace of God.

3 Like the summer breezes playing,
　like the tall trees softly swaying,
　like the lips of silent praying
　　is the perfect peace of God.

4 Like the morning sun ascended,
　like the scents of evening blended,
　like a friendship never ended
　　is the perfect peace of God.

5 Like the azure ocean swelling,
　like the jewel all-excelling,
　far beyond our human telling
　　is the perfect peace of God.

44/45 From Psalm 139
© Christopher Idle/Jubilate Hymns

1 Lord all-knowing, you have found me;
　every secret thought and word:
　all my actions, all my longings
　you have seen and you have heard.

2 Lord almighty, you have made me,
　fashioned me to keep your laws;
　your design and your creation –
　every part of me is yours.

3 Lord all-holy, you have judged me
　by a standard true and right;
　all the best I have to offer
　withers in your burning light.

4 Lord all-loving, you have saved me
　in supreme and mighty grace;
　by your Son's triumphant mercy,
　suffering, dying in my place.

5 Lord all-glorious, you receive me
　where your ransomed servants sing;
　you have spoken, rescued, conquered,
　Christ, our prophet, priest, and king!

46 From Psalm 37
© Michael Perry/Jubilate Hymns

1 Commit your way to God the Lord –
　your cause will shine as bright as fire;
　delight to do God's holy word
　and you shall find what you desire.

2 Be still before the Lord and wait,
　and do not fret when wrong succeeds;
　refrain from anger, turn from hate,
　for God will punish evil deeds.

3 Salvation comes from God alone –
　the faithful know their help is sure;
　to heaven all our needs are known,
　and in God's strength we are secure.

4 Commit your way to God the Lord,
　to peace and truth and grace aspire:
　then mercy shall be your reward,
　God's promises your heart's desire.

47 From Psalm 17
© David Mowbray/Jubilate Hymns

1 Lord of all my footsteps,
　　watching from above,
　keep me in the safety
　　of your perfect love.

2 Others moved by malice
　　spread untruths around:
　shall their schemes not falter
　　and their plans rebound?

3 For their hope is riches
　　time will yet destroy;
　you are all my treasure
　　and my lasting joy.

48
From Psalm 15
© David Preston/Jubilate Hymns

1 Lord, who may venture where you dwell,
or worship on your holy hill?
The pure in heart, whose spotless lives
by word and deed obey your will.

2 They never do their neighbour wrong,
and utter no malicious word;
the sinner's folly they despise,
but honour those who fear the Lord.

3 They keep their oath at any cost,
and gladly lend, but not for gain;
they hate all bribery: come what may,
secure for ever they remain.

49
From Luke 1 (*The Song of Mary*/*Magnificat*)
© Christopher Idle/Jubilate Hymns

1 My soul proclaims
the greatness of the Lord,
and my spirit sings for joy
to my saviour God!
His lowly slave he looked upon in love:
they will call me happy now,
for mighty are the works he has done,
and holy is his name!

2 In every age, for those who fear the Lord
come his mercy,
and the strength of his mighty arm;
he routs the proud,
throws monarchs off their thrones,
while he lifts the lowly high,
fills hungry souls with food,
and the rich sends empty away.

3 To Israel his servant he brings help,
and the promise to our fathers
is now fulfilled:
for Christ has come according to his word,
and the mercy that he showed
to Abraham is now
for his children's children evermore.

50 © Christopher Idle/Jubilate Hymns

1 My Lord, you wore no royal crown;
you did not wield the powers of state,
nor did you need a scholar's gown
or priestly robe, to make you great.

2 You never used a killer's sword
to end an unjust tyranny;
your only weapon was your word,
for truth alone could set us free.

3 You did not live a world away
in hermit's cell or desert cave,
but felt our pain and shared each day
with those you came to seek and save.

4 You made no mean or cunning move,
chose no unworthy compromise,
but carved a track of burning love
through tangles of deceit and lies.

5 You came unequalled, undeserved,
to be what we were meant to be;
to serve instead of being served,
to pay for our perversity.

6 So when I stumble, set me right;
command my life as you require;
let all your gifts be my delight
and you, my Lord, my one desire.

51
From Philippians 2 (*The Songs of Christ's Glory*)
© Brian Black and Word & Music/
Jubilate Hymns

1 Before the heaven and earth
were made by God's decree,
the Son of God all-glorious dwelt
in God's eternity.

2 Though in the form of God
and rich beyond compare,
he did not think to grasp his prize;
nor did he linger there.

3 From heights of heaven he came
to this world full of sin,
to meet with hunger, hatred, hell,
our life, our love to win.

4 The Son became true Man
and took a servant's role;
with lowliness and selfless love
he came, to make us whole.

5 Obedient to his death –
that death upon a cross,
no son had ever shown such love,
nor father known such loss.

6 To him enthroned on high,
by angel hosts adored,
all knees shall bow, and tongues confess
that Jesus Christ is Lord.

52
© Christopher Porteous/Jubilate Hymns

1 He gave his life in selfless love,
    for sinners once he came;
he had no stain of sin himself
    but bore our guilt and shame:
he took the cup of pain and death,
    his blood was freely shed;
we see his body on the cross,
    we share the living bread.

2 He did not come to call the good
    but sinners to repent;
it was the lame, the deaf, the blind
    for whom his life was spent:
to heal the sick, to find the lost –
    it was for such he came,
and round his table all may come
    to praise his holy name.

3 They heard him call his Father's name –
    then 'Finished!' was his cry;
like them we have forsaken him
    and left him there to die:
the sins that crucified him then
    are sins his blood has cured;
the love that bound him to a cross
    our freedom has ensured.

4 His body broken once for us
    is glorious now above;
the cup of blessing we receive,
    a sharing of his love:
as in his presence we partake,
    his dying we proclaim
until the hour of majesty
    when Jesus comes again.

53
From John 6 and 15
© Brian Hoare/Jubilate Hymns

1 I am the Bread,
The Bread of Life;
who comes to me will never hunger.
I am the Bread,
the Bread of heaven;
who feeds on me will never die.
    And as you eat, remember me –
    my body broken on the tree:
    my life was given to set you free,
    and I'm alive for evermore.

2 I am the Vine,
the living Vine;
apart from me you can do nothing.
I am the Vine,
the real Vine:
abide in me and I in you.

    And as you drink, remember me –
    my blood was shed upon the tree:
    my life was given to set you free,
    and I'm alive for evermore.

3 So eat this bread,
and drink this wine,
and as you do, receive this life of mine.
All that I am I give to you,
that you may live for evermore.

54
© Michael Perry/Jubilate Hymns

1 O God beyond all praising,
    we worship you today
and sing the love amazing
    that songs cannot repay;
for we can only wonder
    at every gift you send,
at blessings without number
    and mercies without end:
we lift our hearts before you
    and wait upon your word,
we honour and adore you,
    our great and mighty Lord.

2 The flower of earthly splendour
    in time must surely die,
its fragile bloom surrender
    to you the Lord most high;
but hidden from all nature
    the eternal seed is sown –
though small in mortal stature,
    to heaven's garden grown:
for Christ the Man from heaven
    from death has set us free,
and we through him are given
    the final victory!

3 Then hear, O gracious Saviour,
    accept the love we bring,
that we who know your favour
    may serve you as our king;
and whether our tomorrows
    be filled with good or ill,
we'll triumph through our sorrows
    and rise to bless you still:
to marvel at your beauty
    and glory in your ways,
and make a joyful duty
    our sacrifice of praise.

Verse 2 is specific to 1 Corinthians 15
and may be omitted.

55

From Matthew 27 etc.
© Christopher Idle/Jubilate Hymns

1 He stood before the court
on trial instead of us;
he met its power to hurt,
condemned to face the cross:
our king, accused
of treachery;
our God, abused
for blasphemy!

2 These are the crimes that tell
the tale of human guilt;
our sins, our death, our hell –
on these the case is built:
to this world's powers
their Lord stays dumb;
the guilt is ours,
no answers come.

3 The sentence must be passed,
the unknown prisoner killed;
the price is paid at last,
the law of God fulfilled:
he takes our blame,
and from that day
the accuser's claim
is wiped away.

4 Shall we be judged and tried?
In Christ our trial is done;
we live, for he has died,
our condemnation gone:
in Christ are we
both dead and raised,
alive and free –
his name be praised!

56

© Michael Perry/Jubilate Hymns

1 The hands of Christ, the caring hands,
they nailed them to a cross of wood;
the feet that climbed the desert road
and brought the news of peace with God,
they pierced them through.

2 The kingly Christ, the saviour-king,
they ringed his head with briars woven;
the lips that freely spoke of heaven,
that told the world of sins forgiven,
they mocked with wine.

3 Too late for life, in death too late
they tried to maim him with a spear;
for sacrilege they could not bear –
the sabbath comes, so they must tear
the heart from God.

4 To him be praise, all praise to him
who died upon the cross of pain;
whose agonies were not in vain –
for Christ the Lord is risen again
and brings us joy!

57

© Timothy Dudley-Smith

1 A purple robe, a crown of thorn,
a reed in his right hand;
before the soldiers' spite and scorn
I see my saviour stand.

2 He bears between the Roman guard
the weight of all our woe;
a stumbling figure bowed and scarred
I see my saviour go.

3 Fast to the cross's spreading span,
high in the sun-lit air,
all the unnumbered sins of man
I see my saviour bear.

4 He hangs, by whom the world was made,
beneath the darkened sky;
the everlasting ransom paid,
I see my saviour die.

5 He shares on high his Father's throne
who once in mercy came;
for all his love to sinners shown
I sing my saviour's name.

58

© Michael Saward/Jubilate Hymns

1 Lord of the cross of shame,
set my cold heart aflame
with love for you,
my saviour and my master;
who on that lonely day
bore all my sins away,
and saved me from the judgment
and disaster.

2 Lord of the empty tomb,
born of a virgin's womb,
triumphant over death, its power defeated;
how gladly now I sing
your praise, my risen king,
and worship you,
in heaven's splendour seated.

3 Lord of my life today,
teach me to live and pray
as one who knows the joy of sins forgiven;
so may I ever be,
now and eternally,
one with my fellow-citizens in heaven.

59
From John 20
© Michael Perry/Jubilee Hymns

1 Comes Mary to the grave;
no singing bird has spoken,
nor has the world awoken,
and in her grief all love lies lost
and broken.

2 Says Jesus at her side,
no longer Jesus dying,
'Why, Mary, are you crying?'
She turns, with joy, 'My Lord! my love!'
replying.

3 With Mary on this day
we join our voices praising
the God of Jesus' raising,
and sing the triumph of that love
amazing.

60
From *Exsultet* (Easter Song of praise)
© Christopher Idle/Jubilee Hymns

1 Exult, creation round God's throne!
All heaven, rejoice! All angels, sing!
Salvation's trumpet sound aloud
for Jesus Christ, our risen king.

2 Exult, O earth, in radiant hope;
in Christ's majestic splendour shine!
The Lord is here, the victory won,
the darkness drowned in light divine.

3 Exult, all Christians, one in praise
with our Jerusalem above!
This roof shall ring with Easter songs
that echo Christ's redeeming love.

Optional verse

Exult in God, pure well of truth;
in Christ, fresh fountainhead of grace;
in Spirit, flowing stream of life –
eternal Joy our hearts embrace.

61
From Psalm 18
© Christopher Idle/Jubilee Hymns

1 I love you, O Lord, you alone,
my refuge on whom I depend;
my maker, my saviour, my own,
my hope and my trust without end.
The Lord is my strength and my song,
defender and guide of my ways;
my master to whom I belong,
my God who shall have all my praise.

2 The dangers of death gathered round,
the waves of destruction came near;
but in my despairing I found
the Lord who released me from fear.
I called for his help in my pain,
to God my salvation I cried;
he brought me his comfort again,
I live by the strength he supplied.

3 The earth and the elements shake
with thunder and lightning and hail;
the cliffs and the mountaintops break
and mortals are feeble and pale.
His justice is full and complete,
his mercy to us has no end;
the clouds are a path for his feet,
he comes on the wings of the wind.

4 My hope is the promise he gives,
my life is secure in his hand;
I shall not be lost, for he lives!
He comes to my aid – I shall stand!
Lord God, you are powerful to save,
your Spirit will spur me to pray;
your Son has defeated the grave:
I trust and I praise you today!

62
From *The Easter Anthems*
© David Mowbray/Jubilee Hymns

1 Now lives the Lamb of God,
our Passover, the Christ,
who once with nails and wood
for us was sacrificed:
    Come, keep the feast,
    the anthem sing
    that Christ indeed
    is Lord and king!

2 Now risen from the dead
Christ never dies again;
in us, with Christ as head,
sin nevermore shall reign:
    Come, keep the feast . . .

3 In Adam all must die,
forlorn and unforgiven;
in Christ all come alive,
the second Man from heaven.
    Come, keep the feast . . .

4 Give praise to God alone
who life from death can bring;
whose mighty power can turn
the winter into spring:
    Come, keep the feast . . .

63 © Timothy Dudley-Smith

1 Name of all majesty,
   fathomless mystery,
   king of the ages
   by angels adored;
   power and authority,
   splendour and dignity,
   bow to his mastery –
      Jesus is Lord!

2 Child of our destiny,
   God from eternity,
   love of the Father
   on sinners outpoured;
   see now what God has done
   sending his only Son,
   Christ the beloved One –
      Jesus is Lord!

3 Saviour of Calvary,
   costliest victory,
   darkness defeated
   and Eden restored;
   born as a man to die,
   nailed to a cross on high,
   cold in the grave to lie –
      Jesus is Lord!

4 Source of all sovereignty,
   light, immortality,
   life everlasting
   and heaven assured;
   so with the ransomed, we
   praise him eternally,
   Christ in his majesty –
      Jesus is Lord!

64 © Michael Saward/Jubilate Hymns

1 Christ triumphant, ever reigning,
   Saviour, Master, King!
   Lord of heaven, our lives sustaining,
   hear us as we sing:
      Yours the glory and the crown,
      the high renown,
      the eternal name!

2 Word incarnate, truth revealing,
   Son of Man on earth!
   power and majesty concealing
   by your humble birth:
      Yours the glory . . .

3 Suffering servant, scorned, ill-treated,
   victim crucified!
   death is through the cross defeated,
   sinners justified:
      Yours the glory . . .

4 Priestly king, enthroned for ever
   high in heaven above!
   sin and death and hell shall never
   stifle hymns of love:
      Yours the glory . . .

5 So, our hearts and voices raising
   through the ages long,
   ceaselessly upon you gazing,
   this shall be our song:
      Yours the glory . . .

65 From Psalm 96
© Stephen Horsfall/Jubilate Hymns

1 Sing a new song of glory and salvation,
   through all the earth
      let voices now be raised;
   speak of God's mighty power
      in every nation –
   great is the Lord,
      and greatly to be praised!

2 Sing and adore, shout loud with jubilation,
   tell of the truth and splendour
      of that Name;
   come, bow in worship,
      all of God's creation –
   praise be to God for evermore the same!

3 Say to the earth:
      God's rule is never-ending,
   soon Christ shall come
      to judge our human race –
   anthems of joy
      from earth and heaven blending
   as all creation joins to sing God's grace!

66 From Romans 8
© Michael Perry/Jubilate Hymns

1 He lives in us, the Christ of God,
      his Spirit joins with ours;
   he brings to us the Father's grace
      with powers beyond our powers.
   And if enticing sin grows strong,
      when human nature fails,
   God's Spirit in our inner self
      fights with us, and prevails.

2 Our pangs of guilt and fears of death
    are Satan's stratagems –
by Jesus Christ who died for us
    God pardons: who condemns?
And when we cannot feel our faith,
    nor bring ourselves to pray,
the Spirit pleads with God for us
    in words we could not say.

3 God gave the Son to save us all –
    no greater love is known!
And shall that love abandon us
    who have become Christ's own?
For God has raised him from the grave,
    in this we stand assured;
so none can tear us from the love
    of Jesus Christ our Lord.

67 © Christopher Idle/Jubilate Hymns
    Spirit of holiness,
    wisdom and faithfulness,
    wind of the Lord,
    blowing strongly and free;
    strength of our serving
    and joy of our worshipping –
    Spirit of God,
    bring your fulness to me!

1 You came to interpret
        and teach us effectively
    all that the Saviour
        has spoken and done;
    to glorify Jesus
        is all your activity –
    Promise and Gift
        of the Father and Son:
    Spirit of holiness . . .

2 You came with your gifts
        to supply all our poverty,
    pouring your love
        on the church in her need;
    you came with your fruit
        for our growth to maturity,
    richly refreshing the souls
        that you feed:
    Spirit of holiness . . .

68 © Paul Wigmore/Jubilate Hymns
1 May we, O Holy Spirit, bear your fruit –
    your joy and peace
        pervade each word we say;
    may love become of life the very root,
    and grow more deep and strong
        with every day.

2 May patience
        stem the harmful word and deed,
    and kindness
        seek the good among the wrong;
    may goodness far beyond our lips proceed,
    as manifest in action as in song.

3 May faithfulness endure, yet as we grow
    may gentleness lend courage to the weak;
    and in our self-restraint help us to know
        the grace
            that made the King of Heaven meek.

69 From Psalm 93
© Michael Saward/Jubilate Hymns
1 Clothed in kingly majesty,
    robed in regal power,
        God is over all.

2 Lord of all, unshakeable,
    throned beyond all time,
        God is over all.

3 Greater than the river's roar
    and the surging sea,
        God is over all.

4 Changeless as his law's decrees,
    crowned our holy king,
        God is over all.

70 From *Great and Wonderful*
© Christopher Idle/Jubilate Hymns
1 Great and wonderful your deeds,
    God from whom all power proceeds;
    true and right are all your ways –
    who shall not give thanks and praise?
        To your name be glory!

2 King of nations, take your crown!
    Every race shall soon bow down.
    Holy God and Lord alone,
    justice in your deeds is shown;
        all have seen your glory.

3 To the one almighty God,
    to the Lamb who shed his blood,
    to the Spirit now be given
    by the hosts of earth and heaven
        love and praise and glory!

71 © Christopher Idle/Jubilate Hymns

1 My Lord of light who made the worlds,
  in wisdom you have spoken;
  but those who heard your wise commands
  your holy law have broken.

2 My Lord of love who knew no sin,
  a sinner's death enduring:
  for us you wore a crown of thorns,
  a crown of life securing.

3 My Lord of life who came in fire
  when Christ was high ascended:
  your burning love is now released,
  our days of fear are ended.

4 My Lord of lords, one Trinity,
  to your pure name be given
  all glory now and evermore,
  all praise in earth and heaven.

72 From the Orthodox Lenten Triodion
© Michael Saward/Jubilate Hymns

1 O Trinity, O Trinity,
    the uncreated One;
  O Unity, O Unity
    of Father, Spirit, Son:
  you are without beginning,
  your life is never-ending;
    and though our tongues
    are earthbound clay,
    light them with flaming fire today.

2 O Majesty, O Majesty,
    the Father of our race;
  O Mystery, O Mystery,
    we cannot see your face:
  your justice is unswerving,
  your love is overpowering;
    and though our tongues . . .

3 O Virgin-born, O Virgin-born,
    of humankind the least;
  O Victim torn, O Victim torn,
    both spotless lamb and priest:
  you died and rose victorious,
  you reign above all-glorious;
    and though our tongues . . .

4 O Wind of God, O Wind of God,
    invigorate the dead;
  O Fire of God, O Fire of God,
    your burning radiance spread:
  your fruit our lives renewing,
  your gifts, the church transforming;
    and though our tongues . . .

5 O Trinity, O Trinity,
    the uncreated One;
  O Unity, O Unity
    of Father, Spirit, Son:
  you are without beginning,
  your life is never-ending;
    and though our tongues . . .

73 From Psalm 47
© David Mowbray/Jubilate Hymns

1 Take heart and praise our God –
  rejoice and clap your hands –
  whose power our foe subdued,
  whose mercy ever stands:
    let trumpets sound and people sing,
    the Lord through all the earth is king!

2 Take heart, but sing with fear,
  exalt God's worthy Name –
  with mind alert and clear
  Love's providence aclaim:
    let trumpets sound . . .

3 Take heart for future days,
  for tasks as yet unknown –
  the God whose name we praise
  is seated on the throne:
    let trumpets sound . . .

4 Take heart and trust in God
  the Father and the Son –
  God is our strength and shield,
  the Spirit guides us on:
    let trumpets sound . . .

74 © Michael Saward/Jubilate Hymns

1 This is the truth which we proclaim,
  God makes a promise firm and sure;
  marked by this sign made in that name,
  here, for our sickness, God's own cure.

2 This is the grave in which we lie:
  pierced to the heart by sin's sharp sword,
  risen with Christ, to self we die,
  and live to praise our reigning Lord.

3 This is the sacrament of birth:
  sealed by a Saviour's death for sin,
  trust in his mercy, all on earth,
  open your hearts and let him in!

4 This is the covenant of grace –
  God to the nations offers love;
  people of every tribe and race,
  born by the Spirit from above.

5 This is the badge we proudly wear:
washed by our God, the Three-in-One;
welcomed in fellowship, we share
hope of eternal life begun.

75
From *Saviour of the world*
© Christopher Idle/Jubilate Hymns

1 Jesus, Saviour of the world,
you have bought your people's freedom
by your cross, your life laid down:
now bring in your glorious kingdom.
Come to help us!

2 Christ, who once on Galilee
came to your disciples' rescue:
we, like them, cry out for help –
free us from our sins, we ask you.
Come to save us!

3 Lord, make known your promised power;
show yourself our strong deliverer:
so our prayer shall turn to praise –
hear us, stay with us for ever.
Come to rule us!

4 When you come, Lord Jesus Christ,
filling earth and heaven with wonder,
come to make us one with you –
heirs of life, to reign in splendour.
Alleluia!

76/77
From Psalm 133, J E Seddon (1915–1983)
© Mrs M Seddon/Jubilate Hymns

1 How good a thing it is,
how pleasant to behold,
when all God's people live at one,
the law of love uphold!

2 As perfume, by its scent,
breathes fragrance all around,
so life itself will sweeter be
where unity is found.

3 And like refreshing dew
that falls upon the hills,
true union sheds its gentle grace,
and deeper love instills.

4 God grants the choicest gifts
to those who live in peace;
to them such blessings shall abound
and evermore increase.

78
From 1 Peter 2, J E Seddon (1915–1983)
© Mrs M Seddon/Jubilate Hymns

1 Church of God, elect and glorious,
holy nation, chosen race;
called as God's own special people,
royal priests and heirs of grace:
know the purpose of your calling,
show to all God's mighty deeds;
tell of love which knows no limits,
grace which meets all human needs.

2 God has called you out of darkness
into this most marvellous light;
bringing truth to life within you,
turning blindness into sight:
let your light so shine around you
that God's name is glorified;
and all find fresh hope and purpose
in Christ Jesus crucified.

3 Once you were an alien people,
strangers to God's heart of love;
Christ has brought you home in mercy,
citizens of heaven above:
let his love flow out to others,
let them feel the Saviour's care;
that they too may know his welcome
and his countless blessings share.

4 Church of God, elect and holy,
be the people Christ intends;
strong in faith and swift to answer
each command your master sends:
royal priests, fulfill your calling
through your sacrifice and prayer;
give your lives in joyful service –
sing his praise, his love declare.

79
J E Seddon (1915–1983)
© Mrs M Seddon/Jubilate Hymns

1 Go forth and tell!
O church of God, awake!
God's saving news
to all the nations take;
proclaim Christ Jesus,
saviour, Lord, and king,
that all the world
his worthy praise may sing.

2 Go forth and tell!
God's love embraces all,
and will in grace
respond to all who call:
how shall they call
if they have never heard
the gracious invitation of the Word?

3 Go forth and tell!
    where still the darkness lies;
in wealth or want,
    the sinner surely dies:
give us, O Lord,
    concern of heart and mind,
a love like yours
    which cares for humankind.

4 Go forth and tell!
    The doors are open wide:
share God's good gifts –
    let no one be denied;
live out your life
    as Christ your Lord shall choose,
your ransomed powers
    for his sole glory use.

5 Go forth and tell!
    O church of God, arise!
go in the strength
    which Christ your Lord supplies;
go till all nations
    his great name adore
and serve him, Lord and king
    for evermore.

80/81

1 We give God thanks for those who knew
the touch of Jesus' healing love;
they trusted him to make them whole,
to give them peace, their guilt remove.

2 We offer prayer for all who go
relying on God's grace and power,
to help the anxious and the ill,
to heal their wounds, their lives restore.

3 We dedicate our skills and time
to those who suffer where we live,
to bring such comfort as we can
to meet their need, their pain relieve.

4 So Jesus' touch of healing grace
lives on within our willing care;
by thought and prayer and gifts we prove
his mercy still, his love we share.

82

1 With loving hands,
at work among the suffering
and broken hearts, he ministers,
who is their king.

2 With wounded hands,
outstretched upon a cruel tree,
he lies and then is lifted up
in agony.

3 With pleading hands,
towards the world he longs to bless,
he waits, with heaven's life to fill
our emptiness.

83 From 1 Kings 8

1 God of light and life's creation,
reigning over all supreme,
daunting our imagination,
prospect glorious yet unseen:
    Lord, whom earth and heaven obey,
    turn towards this house today!

2 God of alien, God of stranger,
named by nations of the earth;
poor and exile in a manger,
God of harsh and humble birth:
    let us all with love sincere
    learn to welcome strangers here.

3 God of justice in our nation,
fearing neither rich nor strong,
granting truth its vindication,
passing sentence on all wrong:
    Lord, by whom we die or live,
    hear, and as you hear, forgive.

4 God the Father, Son and Spirit,
Trinity of love and grace,
through your mercy we inherit
word and worship in this place:
    let our children all their days
    to this house return with praise!

84 From Psalm 46, after Martin Luther (1483–1546)

1 God is our fortress and our rock,
our mighty help in danger,
who shields us from the battle's shock
and thwarts the devil's anger:
    for still the prince of night
    prolongs his evil fight;
    he uses every skill
    to work his wicked will –
    no earthly force is like him.

2 Our hope is fixed on Christ alone –
the Man, of God's own choosing;
without him nothing can be won
and fighting must be losing:
    so let the powers accursed
    come on and do their worst –
    the Son of God shall ride
    to battle at our side,
    and he shall have the victory.

3 The word of God will not be slow
while demon hordes surround us,
though evil strike its cruellest blow
and death and hell confound us:
    for even if distress
    should take all we possess,
    and those who mean us ill
    should ravage, wreck, or kill,
    God's kingdom is immortal!

86 From Psalm 44
© Michael Perry/Jubilate Hymns
1 We have heard, O Lord our God
the story of your grace;
and how you gave to us this land,
defending us with your right hand
and showing us your face.

2 You are great, O Lord our God,
we trusted in your name;
we did not triumph by the sword,
but through the victory of your word
you put our foes to shame.

3 Yet today, O Lord our God,
the weak – who once were strong –
cry out to you, 'O come, arise,
reveal your light to darkened eyes,
and turn our sighs to song!'

85 'Rhythmic' version
From Psalm 46, after Martin Luther (1483–1546)
© Michael Perry/Jubilate Hymns
1 God is our fortress and our rock,
our mighty help in danger,
who shields us from the battle's shock
and thwarts the devil's anger:
    for still the prince of night
    prolongs evil's fight;
    he uses all skill
    to work his wicked will –
    no earthly force is like him.

2 Our hope is fixed on Christ alone –
the Man, of God's own choosing;
without him nothing can be won
and fighting must be losing:
    so let the powers accursed
    come try do their worst –
    Christ Jesus shall ride
    to battle at our side,
    and he shall have the victory.

3 The word of God will not be slow
while demon hordes surround us,
though evil strike its cruellest blow
and death and hell confound us:
    for though we meet distress,
    lose all we possess;
    those planning our ill
    may ravage, wreck, or kill;
    God's kingdom is immortal!

87 From *Te Deum*
© Timothy Dudley-Smith
1 God of gods, we sound his praises,
highest heaven its homage brings;
earth and all creation raises
glory to the King of kings:
    holy, holy, holy, name him,
    Lord of all his hosts proclaim him;
to the everlasting Father
every tongue in triumph sings.

2 Christians in their hearts enthrone him,
tell his praises wide abroad;
prophets, priests, apostles own him
martyrs' crown and saints' reward.
    Three-in-One his glory sharing,
    earth and heaven his praise declaring,
praise the high majestic Father,
praise the everlasting Lord!

3 Hail the Christ, the King of glory,
he whose praise the angels cry;
born to share our human story,
love and labour, grieve and die:
    by his cross his work completed,
    sinners ransomed, death defeated;
in the glory of the Father
Christ ascended reigns on high.

4 Lord, we look for your returning;
teach us so to walk your ways,
hearts and minds your will discerning,
lives alight with joy and praise:
    in your love and care enfold us,
    by your constancy uphold us;
may your mercy, Lord and Father,
keep us now and all our days!

88
From Psalms 149 and 150
© Michael Perry/Jubilate Hymns

1 Bring to the Lord a glad new song,
children of grace extol your king:
your love and praise to God belong –
to instruments of music, sing!
Let those be warned
who spurn God's name,
let rulers all obey God's word,
for justice shall bring tyrants shame –
let every creature praise the Lord!

2 Sing praise within these hallowed walls,
worship beneath the dome of heaven;
by cymbals' sounds and trumpets' calls
let praises fit for God be given!
With strings and brass and wind rejoice –
then, join our praise in full accord
all living things with breath and voice;
let every creature praise the Lord!

89
From Revelation 7
© Christopher Idle/Jubilate Hymns

1 Here from all nations,
all tongues, and all peoples,
countless the crowd
but their voices are one;
vast is the sight
and majestic their singing –
'God has the victory:
he reigns from the throne!'

2 These have come out of
the hardest oppression,
now they may stand
in the presence of God,
serving their Lord
day and night in his temple,
ransomed and cleansed
by the Lamb's precious blood.

3 Gone is their thirst
and no more shall they hunger,
God is their shelter,
his power at their side;
sun shall not pain them,
no burning will torture,
Jesus the Lamb
is their shepherd and guide.

4 He will go with them
to clear living water
flowing from springs
which his mercy supplies;
gone is their grief
and their trials are over –
God wipes away
every tear from their eyes.

5 Blessing and glory
and wisdom and power
be to the Saviour
again and again;
might and thanksgiving
and honour for ever
be to our God:
Alleluia! Amen.

90
From Revelation 4, 5 (*Glory and honour*)
© Michael Perry/Jubilate Hymns

1 Glory and honour,
wisdom and splendour,
Lord of creation,
are yours alone:
all of earth's creatures
in exultation
sing to the Lamb upon the throne.

2 Once was the ransom
paid for our freedom –
from every nation
with you we reign:
yours be the praises,
high veneration,
worship for evermore. Amen.

91
From Psalm 65
© Michael Saward/Jubilate Hymns

1 The earth is yours, O God –
you nourish it with rain;
the streams and rivers overflow,
the land bears seed again.

2 The soil is yours, O God –
the shoots are moist with dew;
and ripened by the burning sun
the corn grows straight and true.

3 The hills are yours, O God –
their grass is lush and green,
providing pastures for the flocks
which everywhere are seen.

4 The whole rich land is yours
for fodder or for plough;
and so, for rain, sun, soil and seed,
O God, we thank you now.

92

1 Ring out the bells and let the people know
that God is worshipped
    by the church below:
to all around this truth the bells declare –
'Your needs are lifted up to God
    in prayer!'

2 Ring out the bells and let the people hear –
let hearts be open now,
    and faith draw near;
receive the grace that only God can give –
by word and symbol
    feed and grow and live.

3 Ring out the bells and let the people sing
through changing seasons
    to our changeless King:
all perfect gifts arc sent us from above –
respond with praises for such faithful love.

4 Ring out the bells until that glorious day
when death shall die and sin be done away:
then comes our God
    so everyone shall see –
let all the bells ring out in victory!

93 From Psalms 137 and 138

1 By rivers of sorrow
    we sat and remembered
the city of happiness where we belong;
our harps and our melodies
    hung in the branches,
and there our tormentors
    demanded a song!

2 O how shall we sing
    in the anguish of exile –
the songs of the Lord in a far away land?
Jerusalem, see if I ever forget you
till death take my voice
    and the skill of my hand!

3 You daughter of Babylon,
    doomed to destruction,
you people of Edom
    who throw down our walls,
be warned of the judgement
    on you and your children
when blasphemy fails
    and when tyranny falls.

4 And then shall the strings of the harp
    yield their music,
and then shall the tune of our song
    be restored;
and then shall the kings of the earth
    see God's purpose,
the strong, the unquenchable,
    love of the Lord.

Legal Information

Those seeking to reproduce outside North America works in this book which are the property of Jubilate Hymns or associated authors (attributed '. . /Jubilate Hymns') may write to The Copyright Manager, Jubilate Hymns Ltd, 61 Chessel Avenue, Southampton SO2 4DY (telephone 0703 630038). In the United States of America, these same copyrights, along with those of Timothy Dudley-Smith, are administered by Hope Publishing Company, Carol Stream, IL 60188.

A number of publishers of UK Christian music have uniform concessions and rates. There is normally no charge for 'once off' use of an item provided that permission is obtained and proper acknowledgement made in print. Reproduction for permanent use, or re-sale, does attract a small charge in most cases. Details are avaliable from The Copyright Manager, Jubilate Hymns Ltd.

Most of these publishers also combine to offer a licencing scheme for limited term reproduction. Where this is felt to be an advantage, application should be made to the Christian Music Association, Glyndley Manor, Stone Cross, Pevensey, East Sussex BN24 5BS (telephone 0323 440440).

Jubilate Hymns with their associated authors and composers, and Word & Music, are members of the Mechanical Copyright Protection, and Performing Rights Societies. Appropriate application should be made to these bodies as follows: The Mechanical Copyright Protection Society, Elgar House, 41 Streatham High Road, London SW16 1ER (081 769 4400); The Performing Rights Society, 29–33 Berners Street, London W1P 4AA (071 580 5544).

Other Worship Books from Jubilate

Hymns for Today's Church (First Edition) – Words, Music and Words – both casebound

Hymns for Today's Church (Second Edition) – Words limp, Words casebound, Music and Words casebound, Melody and Words casebound, Words Giant print casebound

Church Family Worship – Words casebound, Music and Words casebound, Words limp

Carols for Today – Music and Words casebound, Music and Words limp, Words limp, *Carols for Today: Choir Supplement*

Carol Praise – Music and Words casebound, Words limp, *Carolling* Words Selection limp, *Play Carol Praise*

Let's Praise! – Music and Words casebound, Words limp

The Wedding Book (with the Marriage Service, ASB 1980) – Music and Words casebound, Words limp

Prom Praise Solos – Music and Words limp

Come Rejoice! – Music and Words limp

The Dramatised Bible – GNB and NIV text casebound

Psalms for Today – Music and Words casebound and limp, Melody and Words casebound, Combined Words (with *Songs from the Psalms*) limp

Songs from the Psalms – Music and Words casebound and limp, Combined Words (with *Psalms for Today*) limp

Topical index

Alphabetical index of hymns